Countering Foreign Interference in U.S. Elections

MAREK N. POSARD, HILARY REININGER, TODD C. HELMUS

Sponsored by the California Governor's Office of Emergency Services

NATIONAL SECURITY RESEARCH DIVISION

For more information on this publication, visit www.rand.org/t/RRA704-4

Library of Congress Cataloging-in-Publication Data is available for this publication.
ISBN: 978-1-9774-0672-9

Published by the RAND Corporation, Santa Monica, Calif.

© Copyright 2021 RAND Corporation

RAND® is a registered trademark.

Support RAND
Make a tax-deductible charitable contribution at
www.rand.org/giving/contribute

www.rand.org

Preface

During U.S. political campaigns, Russia might try again to manipulate and divide U.S. voters via social media. This report is the fourth in a four-part series aimed at helping policymakers and the public understand—and mitigate—the threat of online foreign interference in national, state, and local elections.

Given the past and likely extant threats to U.S. elections, the California Governor's Office of Emergency Services (Cal OES) asked the RAND National Security Research Division (NSRD) for research to help analyze, forecast, and mitigate threats by foreign actors targeting local, state, and national elections.

This is the final report in a four-part series on how to counter foreign interference in U.S. elections, with research relevant to the 2020 election cycle conducted from March 5, 2020, to March 1, 2021. The other reports are as follows (and can be found at www.rand.org/nsrd/projects/cal-oes):

- Marek N. Posard, Marta Kepe, Hilary Reininger, James V. Marrone, Todd C. Helmus, and Jordan R. Reimer, *From Consensus to Conflict: Understanding Foreign Measures Targeting U.S. Elections*, Santa Monica, Calif.: RAND Corporation, RR-A704-1, 2020
- William Marcellino, Christian Johnson, Marek N. Posard, and Todd C. Helmus, *Foreign Interference in the 2020 Election: Tools for Detecting Online Election Interference*, Santa Monica, Calif.: RAND Corporation, RR-A704-2, 2020
- Todd C. Helmus, James V. Marrone, Marek N. Posard, and Danielle Schlang, *Russian Propaganda Hits Its Mark: Experimentally Testing the Impact of Russian Propaganda and Counter-Interventions*, Santa Monica, Calif.: RAND Corporation, RR-A704-3, 2020.

This research was sponsored by Cal OES and conducted within the International Security and Defense Policy Center of the RAND National Security Research Division (NSRD), which operates the National Defense Research Institute (NDRI), a federally funded research and development center sponsored by the Office of the Secretary of Defense, the Joint Staff, the Unified Combatant Commands, the Navy, the Marine Corps, the defense agencies, and the defense intelligence enterprise.

For more information on the RAND International Security and Defense Policy Center, see www.rand.org/nsrd/isdp or contact the director (contact information is provided on the webpage).

Contents

Figures and Tables

Figures

Tables

Summary

In this report, the last in a four-part series on the topic, we explore how foreign disinformation efforts on social media are successfully exploiting divisions among Americans and whether public service announcements can help mitigate the damage. The California Governor's Office of Emergency Services (Cal OES) asked the RAND Corporation's National Security Research Division to help analyze, forecast, and mitigate threats by foreign actors targeting local, state, and national elections. This final report addresses two research questions:

1. What do people think and feel about Russian-sourced content during an election year?
2. Could a public service announcement (PSA) affect these views?

To answer these questions, we conducted a series of focus groups and interviews with volunteers from a prior experiment who held favorable or unfavorable views of Republicans or Democrats or no strong views of either. We wanted to hear, in their own words, what focus group participants thought and felt about actual Russian memes and about a PSA warning of disinformation efforts by foreign actors. We also conducted one-on-one interviews with 15 other people who consume news from different types of sources.

Most participants mistakenly assumed that the source of the content they were shown was fellow Americans, not Russia or its proxies. This result suggests that Americans are vulnerable to foreign disinformation. Although many participants had a positive view of a PSA warning about foreign election interference, the announcement tended to become more relevant to them after we explicitly told them they had just viewed partisan content sourced from Russia, suggesting that PSAs might be effective at preventing foreign disinformation from taking hold.

The results detailed in this report support the main contention of our four-part series: that Russia and its proxies are recycling our domestic partisanship at scale by identifying who dislikes whom and then exploiting those divisions. The content that Russia produces and distributes, when effective, tends to elicit partisan reactions from people who might not initially define themselves in political terms (many participants in the initial experiment did not volunteer their political leanings until they were asked).

We recommend that Cal OES take the following steps:

- Monitor online activity for evidence of foreign election interference before domestic political campaigns become active.
- Release a PSA that provides a general, nonpartisan warning to the public repeatedly throughout election cycles.
- Coordinate with social media companies to flag political content for attribution.

Acknowledgments

We would like to thank our sponsors at the California Governor's Office of Emergency Services (Cal OES). We thank Danielle Schlang and her team from the RAND Corporation's Survey Research Group for conducting the focus groups and interviews. We are grateful to Melissa Bauman, whose dedicated work improved the prose of this report. Finally, we thank Christopher Paul of RAND and Alicia Wanless for their thoughtful reviews.

Abbreviations

Cal OES	California Governor's Office of Emergency Services
CISA	Cybersecurity and Infrastructure Security Agency
COVID-19	coronavirus disease 2019
FBI	Federal Bureau of Investigations
LGBT	lesbian, gay, bisexual, and transgender
PAC	political action committee
PSA	public service announcement
RCT	reflexive control theory

CHAPTER ONE

Introduction

This report outlines a strategy to counter foreign interference in U.S. elections. We posit that adversaries are trying to exploit the fault lines that already exist within U.S. society. Although the causes of these fault lines are complex, we observe that they present tactical opportunities for our adversaries to exploit.

Specifically, we observe that some adversaries seek to identify who dislikes whom and then flood the information space to amplify these differences. The ultimate goal of these adversaries is to exploit these opportunities to reduce the probability that Americans from different backgrounds will reach consensus on issues of public concern.

This is the final report in a four-part series on how to counter foreign interference in U.S. elections (Figure 1.1). The California Governor's Office of Emergency Services (Cal OES) asked the RAND Corporation's National Security Research Division to help analyze, forecast, and mitigate threats by foreign actors targeting local, state, and national elections.

To recap, our first report outlines how Russia and other adversaries interfere in U.S. elections (Posard et al., 2020). In it, we argue that Russian information efforts aim to elicit strong reactions and drive people to extreme positions as a way of reducing the probability that consensus will be reached. The second report focuses on who Russia appeared to be targeting on social media during the early part of the 2020 presidential election campaign (Marcellino et al., 2020). That report describes how

Figure 1.1
What This Series Covers

Disinformation Series

PART 1	PART 2	PART 3	PART 4 (this report)
Reviews what existing research tells us about information efforts by foreign actors	Identifies potential information exploits in social media	Assesses interventions to defend against exploits	Explores people's views on falsehoods

Russia uses fake personas (*trolls*) and highly networked accounts (*superconnectors*) to spread a variety of hyperpartisan themes effectively and quickly. In the third report, we describe how we used a survey experiment to test the impacts on the public of political content that was sourced from Russia and its proxies (Helmus et al., 2020). We found that Russia is successful in accomplishing a key objective from its information efforts: eliciting strong emotional reactions and high engagement with hyperpartisan content.

In our research for this final report, we invited a subset of people from our survey experiment to participate in online focus groups or one-on-one interviews. This report addresses two research questions:

1. What do people think and feel about Russian-sourced content during an election year?
2. Could a public service announcement (PSA) affect these views?

We answer both questions in four parts. First, we briefly review studies that informed our research questions, focusing on how group-based differences could create opportunities for adversaries to exploit. Second, we present results from three online focus groups made up of people who previously held positive views of one party and negative views of the other (Democrat or Republican) or held no strong views about either party (whom we refer to as independents). Third, we present results from individual interviews with people grouped by the types of news media that they consume. Fourth, we summarize our conclusions and outline three recommendations, based on these results, for how to mitigate foreign interference in U.S. elections.

This report and the series overall support our main contention that Russia and its proxies are recycling our domestic partisanship at scale (Paul and Matthews, 2016). The content they produce and distribute, when effective, tends to elicit partisan reactions from people who might not initially define themselves in political terms. Most of the people in our sample mistakenly assumed the source of this content was fellow Americans, not Russia or its proxies. Although many of these individuals reported a positive view of a PSA warning about foreign election interference, this announcement tended to become particularly relevant to them after we explicitly told them they had just viewed partisan content sourced from Russia. We recommend that Cal OES (1) monitor online activity for evidence of foreign election interference before domestic political campaigns become active, (2) release a PSA that provides a general, nonpartisan warning to the public repeatedly throughout election cycles, and (3) coordinate with social media companies to flag political content for attribution.

CHAPTER TWO

Background and Methods

A key feature of a democracy is the capacity for diverse groups of people to find consensus on issues of public concern. In the United States, there is no shortage of these issues—or dearth of divided opinions about them. Our foreign adversaries did not create the underlying problems that created these issues, but they might, under the right conditions, exploit these tactical opportunities to further their foreign policy goals. Such exploitation is nothing new. The Soviet Union and its allies, for example, exploited race- and class-based tensions in the United States during the Cold War (Ewing, 2017). One thing that is different today is that adversaries are using social media to execute their tactics.

Background

Previous research from this series outlined how such adversaries as Russia target elections in the United States (Posard et al., 2020), who they appear to be targeting on social media (Marcellino et al., 2020), and the impact of these efforts on Americans (Helmus et al., 2020). We believe that reflexive control theory (RCT) is, in part, the intellectual basis for Russia's recent efforts to interfere in U.S. elections (for more details, see Posard et al., 2020, pp. 3–4). RCT is a formal theoretical research program that first appeared in Soviet military literature during the Cold War. This program describes a way to convey information to others that could lead them to make some predetermined decision (Thomas, 2004). We have proposed that a key feature of Russian information efforts against the United States is to manipulate one group's view of others.

We found evidence of this strategy on Twitter during the 2020 presidential election campaign (Marcellino et al., 2020). This research revealed two types of suspicious accounts whose behaviors match prior efforts by Russia and its proxies to interfere in U.S. elections: *troll* accounts (fake personas spreading hyperpartisan themes), and *superconnector* accounts (highly networked accounts that quickly spread falsehoods). Furthermore, we found that these suspicious accounts targeted both conservative and liberal online communities, amplifying partisan themes and sowing divisiveness.

Using known Russian-origin memes from the 2016 election,[1] our third report conducted a randomized controlled trial to test the impacts of this content on a sample of Americans (Helmus et al., 2020). This third report describes evidence we found that Russian content elicits emotional reactions from users that correlate with their self-reported willingness to publicly "like" and share the content. In addition, telling users that Russia created the content attenuated these reactions.

Building on this prior work, we conducted a series of focus groups and interviews of volunteers from the survey experiment to hear, in their own words, their thoughts and feelings about select Russian memes. We then asked them for input on a general warning about broader information efforts by foreign actors. In the next section, we describe the methods for these discussions.

Methods

The focus groups were completed online via Facebook; we saved the chat transcripts. The individual interviews were telephone calls that we recorded; we then used Amazon Transcribe to auto-transcribe the audio. Two members of the research team checked the accuracy of each auto-transcribed transcript against the audio recording.

Next, we constructed a coding guide for these transcripts that we based on our interview protocol (see Appendix A). We first conducted a trial for coding in which two team members used Dedoose to independently code each of the focus group transcripts. To ensure intercoder consistency, these two team members discussed their coding decisions and streamlined the codes in the coding guide, then conducted three separate coding tests in Dedoose for relevant codes from the individual interviews.[2]

Participants then answered questions about the memes. Figure 2.1 displays three images seen by participants: a conservative Yosemite Sam meme (sourced from Russia), a liberal lesbian, gay, bisexual, and transgender (LGBT) rights meme (sourced from Russia), and a PSA.[3]

---

[1] A *meme*, as originally defined by evolutionary biologist Richard Dawkins, 1976, referred to a behavior or style that spread from person to person. It has since been redefined, according to McCrae, 2017, as "any fad, joke or memorable piece of content that spreads virally across the web, usually in the form of short videos or photography accompanied by a clever caption."

[2] The two coders completed three separate tests using the software package Dedoose, each with different sets of codes. The first coding test focused on self-report political affiliation, initial views of the Yosemite Sam meme, and initial views of the PSA. The second test focused on initial thoughts of the LGBT rights meme, understanding of the PSA, and views of the PSA after knowing that Russia created the memes. The last coding test involved codes related to thoughts on the LGBT meme and who participants thought created the LGBT meme. We estimated intercoder reliability in Dedoose using a pooled Cohen's Kappa for each test, which were 0.78, 0.75, and 0.93 respectively (de Vries et al., 2008).

[3] We selected the Yosemite Sam meme and LGBT rights meme because both elicited the largest partisan response by respondents in our survey experiment.

Figure 2.1
Russian Memes and Public Service Announcement Used in This Study

During the 2020 election season, foreign actors and cyber criminals are spreading false and inconsistent information through various online platforms in an attempt to manipulate public opinion, discredit the electoral process, and undermine confidence in U.S. democratic institutions.

RECOMMENDATIONS

- Seek out information from trustworthy sources, verify who produced the content, and consider their intent.
- Rely on state and local election officials for information about voter registration databases and voting systems.
- View early, unverified claims with a healthy dose of skepticism.
- Verify through multiple reliable sources any reports about compromises of voter information or voting systems, and consider searching for other reliable sources before sharing such information via social media or other avenues.
- Report potential election crimes—such as disinformation about the manner, time, or place of voting—to the FBI.
- If appropriate, make use of in-platform tools offered by social media companies for reporting suspicious posts that appear to be spreading false or inconsistent information about voter information or voting systems.

The sample of participants for our focus groups and individual interviewees are people who completed our survey experiment on Russian disinformation (for more details, see Helmus et al., 2020). Of 1,529 people who completed the second wave of this survey experiment, 897 volunteered to have a follow-up contact for our focus groups or individual interviews (58.7 percent). Of these volunteers, we identified 106 people who met our inclusion criteria for the focus groups and another 441 people who met our criteria for inclusion to be part of our interview sample. We then used quota sampling for both samples and stopped sending invitations after we met our quotas for the focus groups (n = 15) and individual interviews (n = 27).

Sample of Focus Group Participants

Candidates for this sample completed two questions on this survey that asked them how favorably or unfavorably they viewed Democrats and Republicans. Using these answers as our criteria, we constructed three separate focus groups that were held on Facebook in October prior to the 2020 presidential election. Here, we provide descriptions for each of our focus groups:

1. **Republican Group:** This focus group had eight participants. Five reported holding a very favorable view of Republicans and a very unfavorable view of Democrats. Three reported having just a favorable view of Republicans and a very unfavorable view of Democrats.[4]
2. **Democratic Group:** This group consisted of ten participants who reported holding a very favorable view of Democrats and a very unfavorable view of Republicans.
3. **Independent Group:** This group had a total of nine participants who reported having neither a favorable nor unfavorable view of Republicans or Democrats.

Sample of Individual Interviewees

No interviewees in this sample participated in our focus groups. In the survey experiment from which these interviewees were drawn, participants were sorted into five distinct groups based on their news consumption types. For the interviews, we selected participants from the following three groups: partisan left, partisan right, and analytical skeptics. The partisan left and right groups were defined by their partisan beliefs; each group represented 13 percent of respondents from our survey experiment. We selected the analytical skeptics because they were the largest of these groups, represent-

---

[4]   There were not enough people from our survey experiment who volunteered for us to follow up with them and who self-reported both very unfavorable views of Democrats on our survey experiment and very favorable views of Republicans. Thus, we adjusted this criteria to include participants self-reporting they held just favorable views of Republicans and a very unfavorable view of Democrats. This decision likely reduced the degree of partisanship within the Republican focus group.

ing 40 percent of respondents in our previous experiment. Descriptions of these groups are as follows (and were used in Helmus et al., 2020, pp. 40–43):

- **Partisan Left:** A majority of members of this group reported getting their news from CNN, the *New York Times*, NPR, and the *Washington Post*. This group is most likely to get its news from a website or app. These participants are most likely to be politically left-leaning and to view the Democratic Party favorably and are least likely to believe that coronavirus disease 2019 (COVID-19) is a conspiracy. This group has the highest share of women, atheists or agnostics, Asians, and people not in the labor force.
- **Partisan Right:** A majority of this group reports getting news from Fox News, Buzzfeed, Fox host Sean Hannity, and *USA Today*. It is the only group for which no single news source was used by more than one-half of the participants. These participants were most likely to get news from far-right outlets, such as the Daily Caller, Breitbart, radio host Rush Limbaugh, and One America News Network (OANN). This group is most likely to get news via social media, to believe COVID-19 is a conspiracy, and to hold a favorable view of the Republican Party. Compared with other types, these participants are younger and less educated, and a higher proportion are men. Members of this group are more likely to be employed, but they have below-median incomes.
- **Analytical Skeptics:** Members of this group were the most common type of participant. Most get their news from *USA Today*, ABC, NPR, *Time*, the *Wall Street Journal*, and BBC. This group is most evenly split in terms of news-consumption format. Those who fall into this group are highly analytic (89 percent had perfect scores on the Cognitive Reflection Test scores, a way to measure a person's ability to engage in analytic thinking). They are also disenchanted with politics (46 percent reported an unfavorable view of both political parties). This group also had the most White participants and the most Black participants, and was largely Protestant, educated, and high-earning.

We interviewed a total of 15 people in October 2020, just weeks before the presidential election. We classified five interviewees as "partisan left," five as "partisan right," and five as part of the "analytical skeptics" group. We recorded the interviews, used Amazon Transcribe to automatically transcribe them,[5] and had two members of the research team independently listen to the recordings and correct transcription errors. In the next chapter, we discuss key themes that emerged from these interviews.

---

[5] Details of the Transcribe software can be found at Amazon, undated.

CHAPTER THREE

Focus Groups of Partisans and Independents

In this chapter, we review the results from online focus groups of people organized according to their self-reported political affiliation (i.e., each group consisted of people who reported holding similar political beliefs).[1] We review key themes from our coding of the transcripts from the focus group discussions.[2]

How Participants Described Themselves

The focus groups occurred in October 2020 at the height of a contentious presidential campaign that would result in the highest voter turnout in more than a century. The first question asked in our focus groups was purposefully general: "In a few words, how would you describe yourself?" Despite the timing, none of our focus group participants described themselves in political terms. Instead, they tended to describe their personality traits (e.g., unselfish, shy, friendly), personal interests (e.g., reading, baking, traveling), or demographic background (e.g., retired, state of residence, age). This suggests that partisanship might not always be at the forefront of people's minds—or at least that political beliefs might not have been salient to how people self-identified during these focus groups.

We then directly asked participants to describe their personal political beliefs. No one in the Republican focus group used party labels to answer this question, instead describing themselves as conservative or libertarian. In the Democratic focus group, one-half of the participants ($n = 5$) used the term Democrat, four described themselves as liberal, and one did not respond to this question. Finally, most participants in the independent focus group ($n = 7$) did not self-identify with a major political party or

---

[1] We note that there could be social desirability bias within our focus groups, leading some participants to express views that they believe will align with others in the group or to not express views that might counter the points made by others.

[2] We coded all responses to questions by participants, which might result in multiple codes applied to the same participant. In some cases, we might double count the same code if a participant gave similar answers to a question at different times during a focus group session.

even an ideology during their session, though one person self-identified as conservative and another as a Democrat.

These results might indicate that people were unwilling to talk about their personal politics at first, possibly because they were uncomfortable sharing them with others in the focus group. We do not believe this is the case, for three reasons. First, the focus groups were held online via chat, not in person or via video or audio calls. This virtual modality likely would reduce the degree of social desirability bias that would exist. Second, these online focus groups also asked participants about their personal politics and to describe pressing issues in their community. Participants in the Republican, Democratic, and independent groups openly discussed their personal political views when asked, including mentioning such sensitive issues as Black Lives Matter, the pandemic, appointment of Supreme Court justices, homelessness, and immigration. This would suggest that participants felt comfortable sharing their political views in a group setting. Third, we used the same interview guide for the focus groups and individual interviews. We found a similar pattern of responses to this question in both the focus groups and the individual interviews.

Russian Memes Elicited Partisan Reactions

The focus groups were first shown a conservative meme sourced from Russia (Yosemite Sam, shown in Figure 2.1) followed by a set of questions about their impressions of the meme.[3] The groups then saw a liberal meme with Russian origins (LGBT United, also shown in Figure 2.1) and answered the same questions for the liberal meme. We then coded these initial responses as negative, neutral, or positive.

The frequency of the responses (Figure 3.1) shows that people reacted more positively to memes that reflected their political beliefs. (The number of responses do not match the number of participants in each focus group because some participants expressed contradictory impressions of the content, did not respond, or expressed the same view at different times during the focus group session.)[4] The frequency of negative responses to the conservative Yosemite Sam meme was highest in the Democratic focus group ($n = 11$); the number of positive reactions to the meme was highest in the

---

[3]   Three participants in our focus group viewed the Yosemite Sam meme during the survey experiment; one person saw the LGBT rights meme in the experiment. See Appendix B for more details on the sampling frame for these focus groups.

[4]   Our unit of analysis for coding are expressions by participants, not the individual participant. Some participants in our focus group and interview samples did not answer the question asked of them, gave answers to a different question, expressed contradictory views in their answers, or gave similar answers to the same question at different times during a focus group session. We assume that most people do not have true "attitudes," but carry partially consistent ideas and considerations that they choose to express. For more details on this assumption, see Zaller and Feldman, 1992.

Figure 3.1
Reactions to Liberal and Conservative Memes Mostly Followed Party Lines

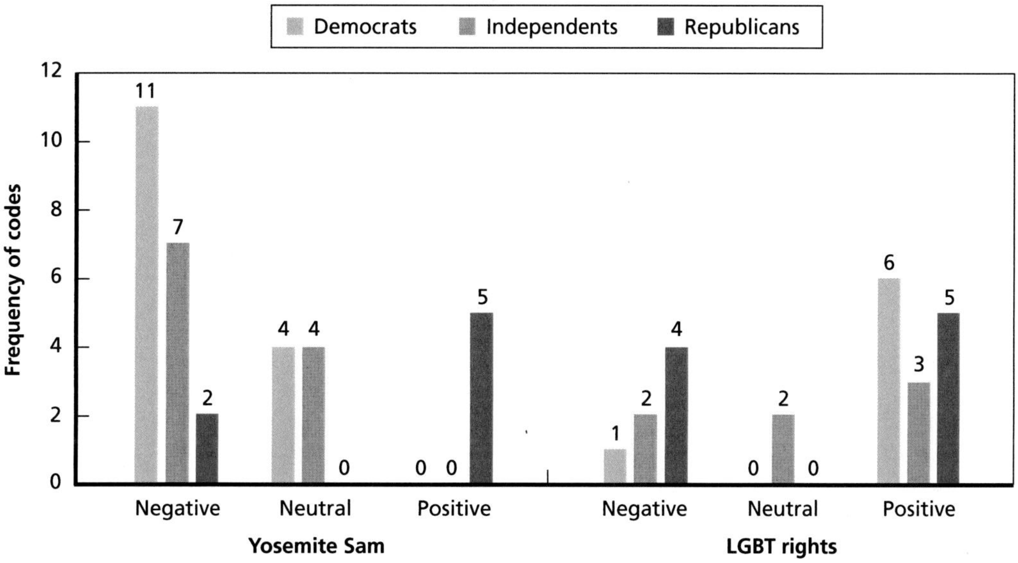

NOTE: Responses by focus group members might have multiple codes.

Republican focus group ($n = 5$). There was less of a partisan divide in reactions to the LGBT rights meme. The Republican focus group was split between negative ($n = 4$) and positive ($n = 5$) reactions. The Democratic group largely responded positively to the LGBT rights meme ($n = 6$), with only one negative response.

Finally, independents' reactions to the conservative Yosemite Sam meme were negative ($n = 7$) or neutral ($n = 4$). Initial reactions to the liberal LGBT rights were divided among negative ($n = 2$), neutral ($n = 2$), and positive ($n = 3$) responses. In general, the patterns in Figure 3.1 support our hypotheses about Russia's goals drawn from our reading of RCT (Posard et al., 2020). It also supports our findings that Russian content does evoke reactions among consumers (Helmus et al., 2020).

Russian Memes Assumed to Come from Domestic Sources

After participants viewed each meme, the focus group moderator asked, "If you had to guess, who created this meme?" We coded the responses three ways: someone in the United States,[5] someone outside the United States, or the respondent did not know. The distribution of the coded responses in each focus group (Figure 3.2) shows that

---

[5]   We applied the code "someone in the United States" if the response suggested individuals or groups were in the United States. For example, if participants answered "conservatives" or "someone frustrated with the turn of our society," we assumed they were talking about Americans unless they explicitly answered a foreign entity.

Figure 3.2
Nearly All Focus Groups Initially Believed That Americans Were Behind the Memes

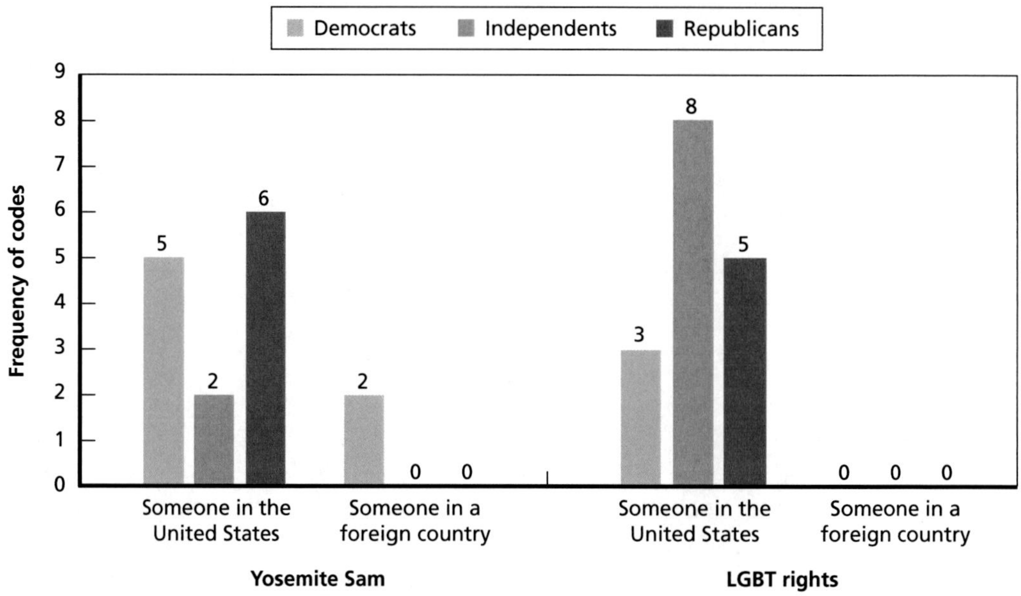

NOTE: Responses by focus group members might have multiple codes.

few participants thought the conservative Yosemite Sam meme was created by someone in a foreign country (*n* = 2), and nobody in any focus group thought the liberal LGBT rights meme was created by someone outside the United States.

We note the vast majority of participants assumed that these memes were sourced from someone in the United States and not in Russia. This finding was surprising because participants had several opportunities to be primed to think that the memes originated from Russia. First, all participants in our focus groups had completed a survey experiment on foreign disinformation three months earlier (in July 2020). Furthermore, some of these same participants viewed these same two memes. Second, during the survey experiment, more than one-half of these focus group participants had already seen a warning label about Russian content, a meme warning them about media literacy, or a video warning about media literacy. Third, the survey experiment told all participants that they had viewed memes sourced from Russia. Fourth, during our focus groups, Facebook displayed a warning label overlaying the conservative Yosemite Sam meme telling viewers that the material contained false information. Facebook did not issue the same warning for the liberal LGBT rights meme despite the fact that both memes were created by Russia and its proxies (U.S. House of Representatives, Permanent Select Committee on Intelligence, 2015–2017). See Appendix B for more details about the content to which participants in the focus groups were exposed during the previous survey experiment.

Understanding and Views of the PSA

Next, we uploaded a PSA (shown in Figure 2.1) that was an abridged version of announcements created by the Federal Bureau of Investigations (FBI) and the Department of Homeland Security's Cybersecurity and Infrastructure Security Agency (CISA) (FBI and CISA, 2020). Before participants viewed the PSA, moderators told them, "Now we are going to show you an example of a public service message from the government. In your own words, what is this PSA trying to tell you?" We then coded responses as evidence of understanding the PSA or not understanding it.

Most people in the focus groups expressed an understanding of this PSA. In the Democratic focus group, eight out of the nine responses showed comprehension of the PSA. In the Republican focus group, four of the six responses demonstrated comprehension. And among independents, eight of the ten responses suggested comprehension of the PSA message.

To illustrate, we coded the following response as understanding the PSA because the respondent discussed content contained in the announcement (i.e., verify sources):

> It reminds consumers that there is a need to self-verify information, as any information seen in the media or other online platforms may be false or spread with an agenda by an outside source.
> —Respondent 9, independent focus group

In contrast, we coded the following response as *not* understanding the PSA because the respondent talked about partisan issues that were not the focus of this announcement (i.e., the campaign of President Donald J. Trump):

> Sounds like Trump's voter squad. To drum up people to stand at the polls and scrutinize everyone who votes.
> —Respondent 3, Democratic focus group

The focus group moderators then asked participants, "What do you think of this public service announcement?" All but two of the 18 responses were positive. Here are two examples of positive responses from people in the Republican and Democratic focus groups:

> I like it a lot. I feel like it's not pushing an agenda or political view. Instead, it's just wanting us to be knowledgeable when we go to vote.
> —Respondent 6, Republican focus group

> In light of today's political environment, I think it is very good information.
> —Respondent 7, Democratic focus group

The two people who expressed negative views of the PSA were both from the Republican focus group. One also had a positive view of the announcement, acknowledging that it served a purpose, even though they saw the announcement as unnecessary:

> It serves a purpose and cannot be discredited but at the same time it is not needed. It reinforces the fear in a more tepid way that a lot of people have succumbed to in this nation.
>
> —Respondent 10, Republican focus group

The other person who expressed a negative view of the PSA believed it was part of a broader conspiracy and mentioned former Secretary of State Hillary Rodham Clinton:

> They are trying to shut down what people see; they want everyone to stick to mainstream media and their lies. They don't want others to open their eyes and see there is some truths from people like Q and Qanon. That's why they ban everything related to that. For example, Hillary's e-mails are being released and media has been quiet about it.
>
> —Respondent 11, Republican focus group

PSA Relevance After Sourcing Revealed

After we asked participants about the PSA, we then told them that these memes were created by the Russian government and people associated with the Russian government, according to research done by the U.S. Senate.[6] Figure 3.3 displays the distribution of codes from our focus groups' responses. The highest number of responses to this question were from Democratic focus group members (n = 7) who believed that the memes were from Russia. Independents were split; most Republicans did not believe that these were Russian memes (n = 5).

Why did some participants not believe that Russia created these memes? Some claimed that they could see no strategic value for Russia to do so. For example, two people from the Democratic focus group told us that they believed Russia could have made the conservative Yosemite Sam meme but were unclear why Russia would create a liberal, pro-LGBT rights meme:

> While the first meme I could see as one that was made by the Russian government, given its aggressive wording and message, the second meme actually surprised me.

---

[6]   This reflects an error in the interview guide that was discovered after the fact—the guide attributed the specific memes to the U.S. Senate. Although both the U.S. House of Representatives, Permanent Select Committee on Intelligence, (2015–2017) and the U.S. Senate (2019) found evidence of Russian interference in the 2016 presidential elections, the House report listed the memes used in the focus groups and individual interviews.

Figure 3.3
Democrats Were More Likely Than Republicans to Believe That Russia Made the Memes

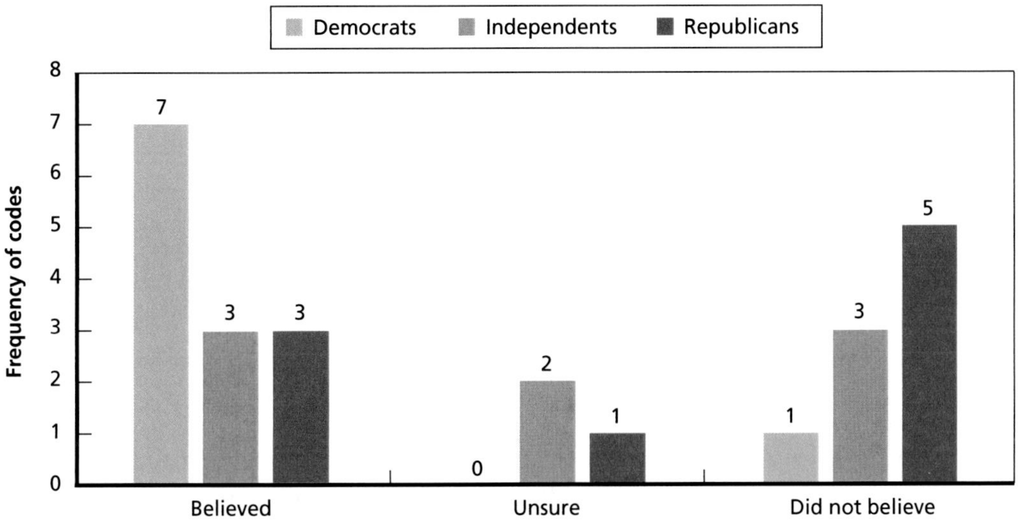

NOTE: Responses by focus group members might have multiple codes.

> I wouldn't think that they would create something that is generally speaking, more positive than negative in message.
> —Respondent 9, Democratic focus group

> I believe Russians created the first meme, but why the second? Russia is always trying to pit people against each other. Are there that many homophobics in our society and are they trying to divide us?
> —Respondent 5, Democratic focus group

Similarly, one member of the Republican focus group was unclear why either meme would help Russia's goals:

> I do not believe Russia created the first meme. The second one, I'd say similar. I don't see how either meme would benefit Russia. Same goes with having Trump or a conservative party in office. Honestly, a conservative President in my mind would be a negative to Russia, not a positive. And no, nothing has changed in my views.
> —Respondent 6, Republican focus group

General frustration with the problem of foreign information efforts was a key reason that some participants held a more negative view of the PSA after learning that the memes they saw were sourced from Russia. For example, two respondents from the Republican focus group suggested that warnings in the PSA merely led them to be skeptical of all information:

It seems all disseminated information, even PSAs, at root are inherently political. Some more than others, but always politically influenced.

—Respondent 8, Republican focus group

Yes, always. I don't think there is anything in this world now without an agenda.

—Respondent 10, Republican focus group

For other participants, the PSA seemed to crystalize the threat of foreign information efforts after we told them that both memes were sourced from Russia:

Knowing the Russian government created the memes makes the PSA feel more real and relevant.

—Respondent 1, independent focus group

I could tell that it was created by the U.S. government. I am reassured to learn that it really was. I am glad the U.S. government is investing in informing and educating the public about voter suppression.

—Respondent 6, Democratic focus group

The focus group moderators then asked participants about the PSA, "Now that you know who created each image, does this change your views of the PSA or the memes?" Most responses to this question (Figure 3.4) indicated no change in their views of the PSA ($n = 16$); seven indicated a more positive view of the PSA; three had a more negative view of it.

Most people who told us their views of the PSA did not change appeared to still believe in the announcement's core message. For example, one Republican participant who initially expressed a positive view of the PSA explained:

Nope, it doesn't change my [positive] views of the PSA or the memes. My beliefs are my beliefs. Memes created by Russia or some other entity won't affect my opinion.

—Respondent 6, Republican focus group

A Democratic participant who initially said it was disappointing that the PSA was needed at all told us:

It doesn't change my views of the PSA. Just shows how necessary it is for people to verify and do their own research.

—Respondent 9, Democratic focus group

Figure 3.4
Identifying Source of Content Had Little Effect on People's Views

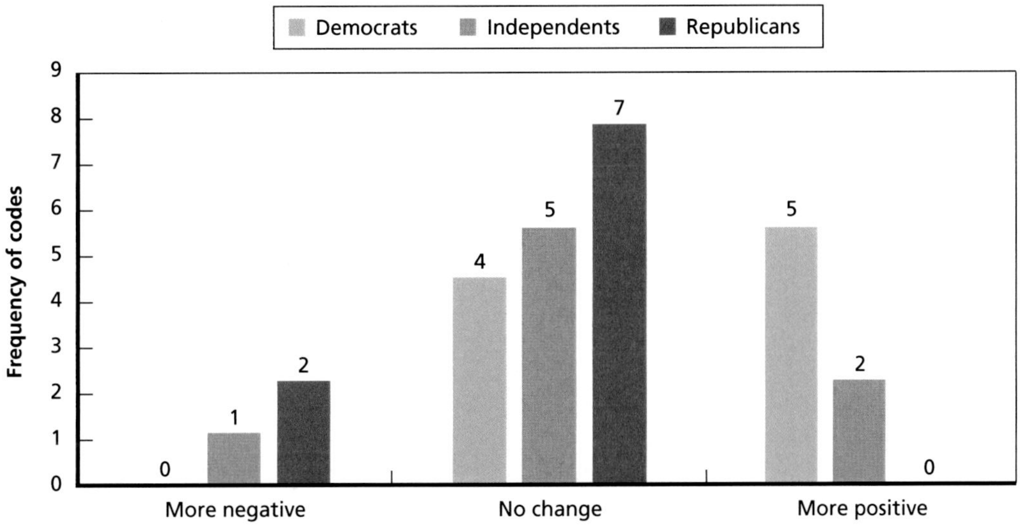

NOTE: Responses by focus group members might have multiple codes.

PSA Might Highlight Threat of Misinformation, Election Security

At the beginning of the focus groups, we asked people to describe the most pressing issue in their communities right now. Most respondents mentioned various domestic issues (e.g., gang activity, homelessness, race relations) ($n = 18$) or the COVID-19 pandemic ($n = 14$). Just two participants mentioned issues that were loosely related to misinformation or election security topics.[7] We asked the same question again as the last query to the focus groups, and coded their responses to these questions again. Although most participants ($n = 15$) said they did not change their answers to this question,[8] seven did mention misinformation or election security–related issues covered in the PSA:

> My comment stands—what I said before—but I also believe that information we receive can be misleading and I feel the media has done a lot of damage by not just reporting information but putting a political bias and has caused a great divide among our citizens because they believe what is being reported and many times that just isn't the case.
>
> —Respondent 3, Republican focus group

---

[7] In the Republican focus group, one participant told us the most pressing issue was that "We live in a culture now that teaches others to repress their views if those views are not the same or in line with the one originating them." A second participant in this same focus group agreed with this statement and then said homelessness was a pressing issue.

[8] Some participants initially said their answers did not change but then said a new issue was also a pressing issue to them.

> We were so naive four years ago about election interference and voter suppression. This type of research will be helpful in strengthening our democracy. Thank you!
> —Respondent 6, Democratic focus group

One person mentioned dissemination of falsehoods and questioned whether we were representatives of the RAND Corporation:

> OK, circling back . . . the right answer is what this is leading to . . . dissemination of false information . . . OK, prove this discussion is not really being created and monitored by a foreign government under the guise of a research company?!
> —Respondent 10, Republican focus group

Summary of Focus Group Results

We conducted three online focus groups with people who reported on a previous survey that they held favorable or unfavorable views of Republicans or Democrats or no strong views of either. The Republican focus group consisted of people who reported favorable views of Republicans and unfavorable views of Democrats; the Democratic group were people who held favorable views of Democrats and unfavorable views of Republicans; the independent group consisted of individuals who held neither favorable nor unfavorable views of both Democrats and Republicans.[9] Their responses revealed five key themes.

First, most people in our focus groups did not initially define themselves in political terms. Second, when we showed them the Russian memes, many of these same people expressed partisan reactions. Third, the vast majority of people in our focus groups assumed that the memes were created by Americans, not a foreign actor, such as Russia. Fourth, most people in our focus groups seemed to understand key points from the PSA and expressed a positive view of it. Finally, this PSA became particularly relevant for some people after we told them that the memes they had just viewed were created by Russia and its proxies (See Appendix C for more details on research surrounding the use of PSAs). In the next section, we review similar results from our individual interviews.

---

[9] As stated in Chapter Two, there were not enough people from our survey experiment who volunteered for us to follow up with them and who self-reported both very unfavorable views of Democrats and very favorable views of Republicans on our survey experiment. Thus, we adjusted this criteria.

CHAPTER FOUR

Individual Interviews

In general, the results from our individual interviews were similar to those of our focus groups. In this chapter, we describe our interviews with a sample of 15 participants, then discuss the five key themes that we coded in transcripts of these interviews.[1]

How Participants Described Themselves

As we did with the focus groups, the first question we asked interviewees was to describe themselves. All 15 interviewees described themselves in nonpolitical terms, such as their personality (e.g., outgoing, caring, introverted), familial or professional roles (e.g., single mother, husband, veteran), demographic background (e.g., race or age), or hobbies (e.g., gardening, art, literature). The two people who did use political terms—one a conservative, and the other a liberal—mentioned their political beliefs in passing, so the nonpolitical descriptors they used to describe themselves appeared more relevant to coders. Again, politics was not a salient topic during the these focus groups at first, just one month before the presidential election.

Russian Memes Elicited Partisan Reactions

We first showed interviewees the conservative Yosemite Sam meme, followed by the liberal LGBT meme (Figure 2.1). We asked interviewees to describe their initial impressions of this content, and coded their responses as positive, neutral,[2] or negative (Figure 4.1). We used more than one code for interviewees who expressed positive and

---

[1] We coded all responses to questions by participants, which might result is multiple codes applied to the same participant. For each individual, we did not count the same code more than once if a participant gave a similar response to the same question at different points during the interview.

[2] The "neutral" code represents responses that described how the interviewees did not have a positive or negative opinion or described the content within each meme. Some participants gave these neutral responses and then expressed a positive or negative view of the same meme later in their answers.

Figure 4.1
Frequency of Codes for Responses to Initial Thoughts of the Conservative and Liberal Russian Memes

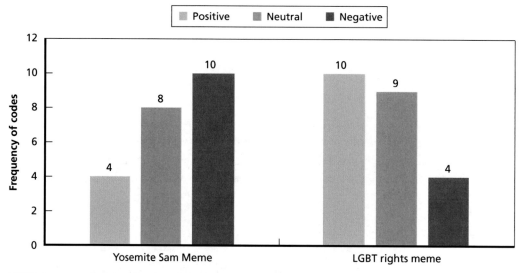

NOTE: Responses by interviewees might have multiple codes.

negative views of the content, or for those who did not have an opinion at first but eventually expressed a definitive view of the memes.

The results illustrated in Figure 4.1 suggest that both memes elicited divisive reactions from some interviewees. For example, four responded positively to the conservative Yosemite Sam meme, eight were neutral, and ten responded negatively. Similarly, the liberal LGBT rights meme elicited ten positive, nine neutral, and four negative responses. In general, the results suggest that some participants are working through their beliefs on sensitive social issues. For example, one expressed several considerations related to firearms when asked about the conservative meme:

> Well, it's kind of, like, upsetting to me. I mean, I did grow up watching Yosemite Sam. I thought it was funny. I mean, I don't know, I don't like guns, but I also don't like the thought of our right to own one taken away from us. I don't like that [loss of rights] more, so I kind of agree with them, but I don't [like guns], so . . .
> —Respondent 1090, partisan right

Others expressed their personal history with the cartoon and guns as they worked through their views:

> I grew up watching his cartoons and my father and my brother both really like them. Also I'm former military and I enjoy target shooting. Mm-hmm, but I don't agree with the [Yosemite Sam] meme on the left. OK, I wouldn't share it.
> —Respondent 42, partisan left

Another interviewee also struggled with contradictions to work through what the LGBT rights meme meant:

> Yeah, I mean the expression on the man, you know, mm-hmm, very . . . it seems kind of inspiring, but my personal beliefs concerning homosexuality as a Christian will come in to say, "Well, you know, they . . ." Yeah, it makes me kind of see also the gulf, like, people who are politicized in terms of gay rights or with somebody who—I guess, this man. You know, you say he is gay, and, um, and just kind of up against the gulf. Well, how would I . . . like, how he might or how the movement might perceive me and my beliefs? Essentially, it is probably a lot more nuanced than he might understand or they might understand. You know, it's not—it's not the black and white—even though there is that side of that. So, and um, yeah, I would say mixed feelings.
>
> —Respondent 176, analytic skeptic

Some respondents worked through contradictions in deciding whether to share the meme, considering its source and meaning:

> I don't know what 'we deserve Equal rights' means at this very point. Like, I don't know what that means, but if I was to be sharing things, I might be likely to share that particular image. But knowing that it's sponsored makes me less likely to share. I try not to share things that are sponsored.
>
> —Respondent 42, partisan left

We also asked interviewees to speculate about "What types of people do you think would like these memes?" The purpose of this question was to understand whether people made broader generalizations about other groups after viewing this content (Posard et al., 2020). We then coded these answers into five groups: people who are pro-gun or pro-LGBT, nobody, everyone, liberals, or conservatives (Figure 4.2). Again, some interviewees gave responses that led to more than one code being applied to their answers. The results suggest a partisan response to the memes: Many interviewees assumed that people who are pro-gun ($n = 5$) or conservatives ($n = 9$) would like the conservative Yosemite Sam meme, and many assumed that people who are pro-LGBT ($n = 2$) or liberals ($n = 8$) would like the LGBT rights meme.

These findings are not surprising given that both Russian memes are targeting social issues that tend to vary by Americans' political beliefs. It does, however, suggest that Russian content is capable of evoking a partisan reaction from people. To illustrate, here are two responses from the same self-described conservative about who would like the conservative and liberal memes:

> I mean, a conservative Republican would love to think this is funny. Um, and someone who believes in God, I would think; uh, and also some probably not-so-good apples that—what do you call those right-wing groups? I forget what they're

Figure 4.2
Participants Were Asked Who Would Like Each Russian Meme

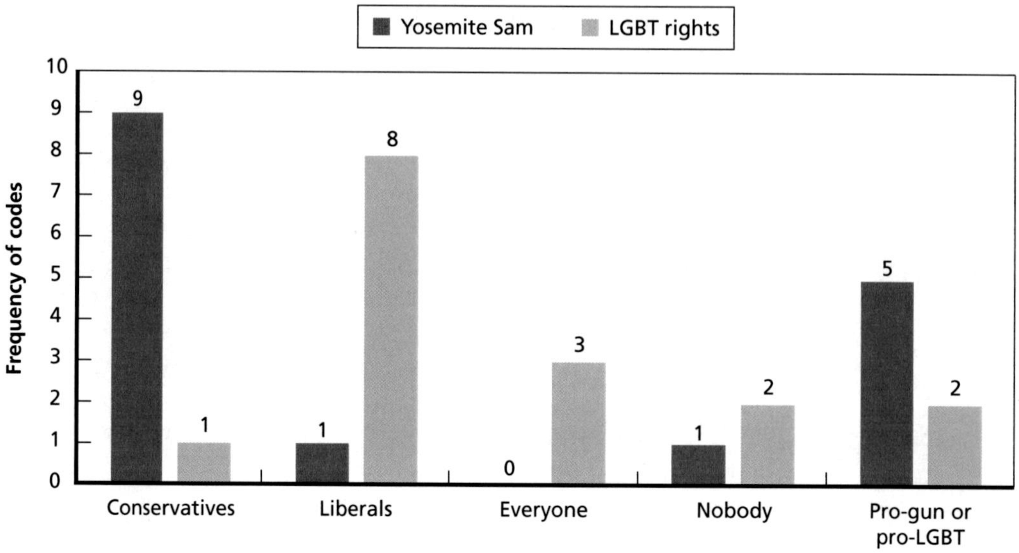

NOTE: Responses by interviewees might have multiple codes.

called. Um, it'll come to me in a minute—they would probably like something like this, but, you know, more of a violent version.

—Respondent 1757, partisan right, on the conservative Yosemite Sam meme

Yeah, well, definitely the LGBT community, of course, because that's who it's supporting, but the very liberal, the liberal media would support this. The liberal politicians. Um, you know, like Kamala Harris and, uh, you know, her group of people. They would support this.

—Respondent 1757, partisan right, on the liberal LGBT rights meme

These quotes highlight how some consumers generalize about how groups of people might respond to the content of the memes. This person assumed that conservatives, Republicans, and violent groups would think the Yosemite Sam meme was funny. This same person assumed that liberals, the liberal media, and liberal politicians would like the LGBT rights meme. Finally, this person extrapolated that then-Senator Kamala Harris and those who support her would also like the LGBT rights meme. Neither of these memes reference a political party, political ideology, the media, politicians, or Vice President Harris.

We also found evidence of this group-based generalizing by someone who self-described themselves as independent but was classified as part of the partisan right news consumption group:

All right. I'm thinking maybe men—um, conservative, middle age, maybe older. I don't know. Maybe middle age, working class, maybe more like a rural, not so much an urban lifestyle. Um, that's what Yosemite Sam makes me think of, you know, independent people. Preppers. You know, people who are living off the grid.
    —Respondent 1090, partisan right, on the conservative Yosemite Sam meme

. . . and the other meme, that I think appeals more to younger people. I don't really see an age group. Well, you know, younger—um, maybe middle to upper class. Um, urban. Since men are shown. I would think of men, but women, too . . . I think it just—a liberal mindset to me is more of a—I don't know, socioeconomic. It's also educated people, people who have gone to school, you know, maybe up through university. OK, I don't know. It's almost like they have more—they use their intellect.
    —Respondent 1090, partisan right, on the liberal LGBT rights meme

These quotes highlight the assumptions that people made about who would like these memes. This interviewee assumed that the Yosemite Sam meme would appeal to men who are middle aged or older, come from rural parts of the country, hold conservative political views, and might live a self-sufficient life off the grid. In contrast, this same person assumed that the LGBT rights meme would appeal to younger people who have higher household incomes, hold college degrees, and have liberal political viewpoints.

Russian Memes Assumed to Come from Domestic Sources

After interviewees viewed each meme, we asked them to guess who created them. We then coded these responses as someone in the United States,[3] someone outside the United States, or the interviewee did not know. Figure 4.3 shows the distribution of these codes, with some responses requiring more than one code.

As the figure shows, the responses indicated that the overwhelming majority of interviewees believed that the memes were created by someone within the United States (n = 14 for the conservative Yosemite Sam meme; n = 13 for the LGBT rights meme). Just three suggested that someone in a foreign country might have created the conservative Yosemite Sam meme, one thought someone in a foreign country might have created the LGBT rights meme, and two people were not sure. Again, several interviewees viewed these same memes during our previous survey experiment, and

---

[3]   As we did with the focus groups, we applied the code "someone in the United States" if the response suggested individuals or groups in the United States. For example, if participants answered "conservatives" or "someone frustrated with the turn of our society," we assumed that they were talking about Americans unless they explicitly answered a foreign entity.

Figure 4.3
Most Interviewees Believed That Americans Created the Two Memes

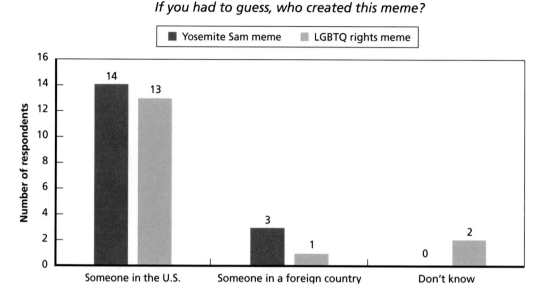

If you had to guess, who created this meme?

the majority had viewed interventions that warned them about foreign disinformation in this survey. Appendix B provides more details about the type of content that our interviewees viewed in our July 2020 survey experiment.

The fact that some memes mentioned or imitated a political activist group seemed to lead some interviewees to believe that the Russian memes were created by U.S. activists. For example, one interviewee speculated that a foreign country might have created the conservative meme but also that a U.S. political action committee (PAC) could have generated this content because this meme displayed a logo for the fictitious group South United:

> Who created? I would have no idea. You know, I think there's a lot of international people that are creating memes to stir up people. Um, I don't know who those people are. But I've heard that that's the case. Um, there are certainly, I think, some people on all parts of the political spectrum that are advertising. You know, some of my family are rural, hardcore Republican people, and I see what they're passing around. I don't even know if they know where it comes from or how much they believe it. . . . so I think it could be some super PAC, but I tend to think, you know, like the super PACs are a little bit smoother. So I would say this is just someone in their backyard because the South United—like, who says that? Or some international type of agent just stirring up stuff.
> —Respondent 2176, analytic skeptic, on the conservative Yosemite Sam meme

Similarly, some interviewees assumed that the LGBT rights meme was created by a U.S. activist group advocating gay rights in the United States. This assumption appeared to be partly based on the meme displaying a logo from the fictitious group "LGBT United" (Ring, 2018).

> Yeah, I do see the LGBT United and so on, so that I know the LGBT, um, you know, this should be proponents of, uh, rights for, um, the LGBT community. And so, you know, that would be their organizing . . . reason for existing. Uh, so in terms of, you know, the perspective on issues—like, this says gay rights. I mean, obviously, they would be the proponents of gay rights. Um, that's probably all of that. All that I can infer about them.
> —Respondent 168, partisan right, on the liberal LGBT rights meme

Understanding and Views of the PSA

After showing interviewees the Russian memes, we then showed them the PSA used in the focus groups. This PSA was based on actual announcements from the FBI and CISA (2020) and featured the agencies' logos. We asked people to describe in their own words what the PSA was trying to tell them to gauge their comprehension of the announcement. We coded their response as "understanding" the PSA if they mentioned a topic contained in the announcement (e.g., disinformation, threats to election by foreign actors, sharing of falsehoods online). All but one person in our interview sample understood the PSA. The interviewee who did not understand it assumed that the PSA was propaganda, trying to instill fear, and designed to control people. This response also referenced Adolf Hitler and mentioned the need to carry a gun.[4] The person did not mention the content described in this PSA.

Next, we asked people to give their initial impressions of this PSA. We coded these responses five ways: positive or negative view of the PSA, neutral view, and negative or positive view of the problems surrounding foreign disinformation (Figure 4.4). None of the responses expressed a positive view of the foreign disinformation problem after viewing the PSA.

The results show that the PSA appears effective for some people in our limited sample. Four responses expressed a positive view of the PSA; four expressed a negative view of the problem surrounding foreign disinformation (even though we did not ask about this problem). For example, one interviewee simply stated, "I think it needs to

---

[4] Author's summary of Respondent 2808 response to the question, "In your own words, what do you think this PSA is trying to tell you?"

Figure 4.4
Frequency of Codes for Responses to Initial Impressions of the PSA

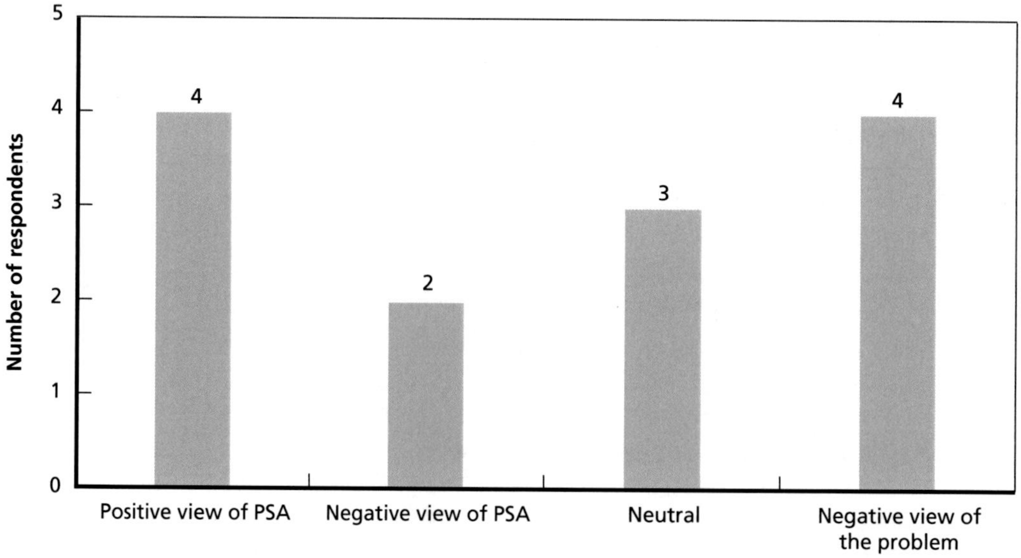

NOTE: Responses by interviewees might have multiple codes.

be spread more widely."[5] Another called the PSA "a good reminder for people to be more . . . critical and suspicious of . . . the media we're consuming."[6]

Other interviewees had a negative response about the general problem of foreign disinformation. This suggests that the PSA effectively led some people to think critically about the threats surrounding foreign disinformation. For example, one interviewee did not have an opinion about the PSA but was scared by the entire issue discussed in the announcement:

> It's kind of scary. It is kind of like the times we're living in a fake news [era]. Uh, just another thing to deal with, in a way. It's weird. I don't know. People are doing stuff like that. It just seems dishonest, kind of, I don't know. It just seems kind of odd. The things that are good enough—you know, good enough. It should just be a straightforward—You shouldn't have to lie about it. Because, like, what's the reason for the deception? You know? Are they trying to do something negative? And what? What's the reason behind it? What are they trying to cause, destabilize, or whatever, trying to do? It's kind of scary, and it's kind of left-staging.
> —Respondent 977, partisan right

---

[5] Respondent 42 response to the question, "What do you think of this public service announcement?"

[6] Respondent 159 response to the question, "What do you think of this public service announcement?"

Another interviewee questioned whether the PSA was from the FBI and then discussed concerns about foreign disinformation from China:

> I mean, to me, I think you get to a certain age and you've been through so much of this stuff that you're just going, you know, "what's going now?" You can't believe anything. I don't even know if this is a true FBI—is a, you know, seal of approval or something. So I would just kind of go, huh? I would just look at it and say, "Well, I already know what I already know," that China's trying to, you know, they've been trying to get involved in on—this has been going on since I've been—freaking in the '60s, you know? So it's nothing new. It's just more, more show time. Um, but if it was coming from them and it's a true statement, then I'm like, yeah, well, I have common sense. I know they've been trying to do this forever. It's just getting more intense as the years go on—and especially this last election with Donald Trump, you know, because so many people dislike him. That, and then since he got into office, it was just, like, I mean, it was unbelievable to a lot of people—as well as me at the time. You know?
>
> —Respondent 1757, partisan right

Two interviewees expressed negative views of the PSA. One interviewee did not believe that the FBI would release this message and thought it was something that President Trump would directly release:[7]

> I just don't believe that the FBI would put that out. It's just—it's completely ridiculous. It's something that Trump would put out, but I don't—just, no, it's just stupid. They didn't put that out.
>
> —Respondent 2808, analytic skeptic

The other person expressed negative views of the PSA at two different points during the interview. At first, the interviewee did not believe that others were trying to spread misinformation about the election. Later in the interview, this same interviewee related the PSA to celebrities and cults but not foreign bad actors.

> I think it's kind of strange. I do think that people will be, like, trying to spread misinformation about the election. But I think the second paragraph doesn't relate at all to the first one, and the second one just sounds way more like, I mean, I'm sure it does happen, but it sounds way less realistic than the first paragraph, which I'm sure will happen . . .
>
> It sounds like they're just, like, talking about celebrities, like, starting cults, and I'm sure that that happens, but I don't think it's necessarily related to, like, trying to not get information or not get wrong information about the election, you know?
>
> —Respondent 993, partisan right

---

[7] This negative response was from the same interviewee who did not appear to understand the PSA.

These quotes highlight a need for any PSA to clearly show that it is from an official government entity, such as Cal OES, the FBI, or CISA. We note that most interviewees recognized the FBI's logo, but the CISA logo was less recognizable. Furthermore, any PSA should be well designed, succinct, and clearly state the threat. This PSA was rather lengthy, and some interviewees might not have completely read the announcement or might not have fully understood all of the details.

PSA Relevance After Sourcing Revealed

After viewing the PSA, we told interviewees that both of the memes that they saw were created by the Russian government and its proxies. Most interviewees believed us ($n = 12$), two were unsure, and one did not believe the memes were Russian. The two who were unsure were skeptical of the claim and needed more details. The one interviewee who did not believe the memes were Russian explained by generalizing about who created the Yosemite Sam meme:

> Well, OK, maybe the one on the left [conservative Yosemite Sam meme], but the one on the right with the gay people, I don't—I don't—No, I just don't believe that they would. I don't know. I'm sorry. I just don't believe it. I, I can't say why. It just doesn't seem plausible. Plausible, plausible. But it, maybe it is. Maybe I'm completely off base here . . . I don't know how to help. It just looks like something that comes from a young, um, disenfranchised white male who loves their guns and hates gay people. That's what it looks like to me. I don't see why the Russians would have anything to do with that. But maybe I'm wrong.
> —Respondent 2808, analytic skeptic

After we told interviewees that the memes they viewed came from the Russian government, we asked whether their views of the PSA changed. Most interviewees ($n = 9$) said that there was no change in their views, which were generally positive. For example, one interviewee whose views did not change said:

> I assumed that it was legitimate, but I wasn't really sure after I learned that the first two were created by the Russian government. No, I think it's a pretty straightforward message that, you know, we should all be aware of.
> —Respondent 177, partisan left

However, six responses suggested a more positive view of the PSA: [8]

---

[8]   Respondent 186 response to the question, "The PSA—third image we talked about—was *not* created by the Russian government. Now that you know who created each image, does this change your views of the public service announcement we are showing you?"

It makes me feel better about it, that it's a legitimate, um, post from our government or a news source or whatever. Puts me a little bit more at ease.

—Respondent 186, partisan left

Some respondents appreciated the PSA more after learning that the memes were Russian and reported seeing a greater use for the PSA:

If [the PSA] had come with these two and say, "both of these were created by Russian government," then I think I would have taken the message a little bit more seriously. Just, like, you know, I think—or, at least, that I felt like—it wasn't giving me any more information. But now I see that, apparently, you know, my view was kind of skewed as well—thinking, you know, mostly the misinformation was related to maybe right-wing extremist groups and the message it might be trying to send; not so much, sort of, to the liberal left.

—Respondent 176, analytic skeptic

Well, I mean, they're trying to avoid you from starting and joining groups and starting controversial content—it says that right there, and hopefully people could read that and kind of say, "you know, we need to stay away from this kind of disinformation and ugliness." Um, so it's kind of a good PSA. Yeah. I mean, I like it at that point, uh, that you could read it, and they're trying to explain it to you. A lot of people are not gonna believe it, no matter what. You know, because there's so many. There's some great people in the FBI, but there's also a lot of bad actors too, and even with CISA agency… So it's kind of, you know, this political season is kind of rough to believe anything.

—Respondent 1757, partisan right

PSA Might Highlight Threat of Misinformation, Election Security

As we did with the focus groups, we asked respondents at the beginning of each interview to name the most-pressing issues facing their community. Most cited COVID-19 ($n = 8$) or various domestic issues ($n = 8$). As also occurred with the focus groups, most did not change their opinion ($n = 10$) when asked this question again at the end. However, five interviewees did report changing their opinion on their community's most-pressing issues.

Honestly, now that I'm like—OK, it's probably the fact that you've made this very salient to me, but, um—the misinformation crisis is probably the most pressing issue, and I probably would have said that to begin with—um, I wasn't really thinking along those lines. But the misinformation crisis is something that affects both sides pretty equally. Um, So, yes, I'm changing my answer to that.

—Respondent 237, partisan left

Just raising the issue of misinformation appeared to affect even long-standing views and caused a few respondents to think about how misinformation affected their deeply held beliefs:

I mean, yeah, I think, you know, you put something on the spot like, what's the most pressing issue? And I'm like, uh—the environment. Because it is to me, at the moment. Then I'm thinking, OK, what has happened in my community lately? And, you know, I feel like coronavirus is going to come and go. We just have to be responsible. So there's that, you know, not the worst thing right now, but the whole, you know, social justice thing I feel is really important. And I see it in my community. But . . . and I know I brought up things, like how . . . I see basically hate speech and hateful memes all the time on, um, in my community postings. So, like, Nextdoor has a lot of that. I am not part of the community postings, um, in my area on Facebook, for the most part, other than the mom groups. Um, but my family is part of in their city, um, part of some community boards and I'll go and read their posts—not my family's postings but the postings in those cases, it's just all, it's my it's my county still, it's all hate speech . . . not all, but it's terrible. So if that . . . and memes like this, honestly, like kind of crazy, crazy things that . . . I can't even imagine who would post them. So maybe this is a big issue or a bigger issue than I thought it was. The disinformation and the election. Um, and all the way that social media is spreading crazy stuff, and it's really to pit people against each other.

—Respondent 186, partisan left

Additionally, six responses cited misinformation as an important issue facing their community after this interview. Although not all who mentioned misinformation said it was the *most* pressing issue, some considered it among the most important. One respondent's views of the most pressing issue did not change, but the person reported a new appreciation for the role of misinformation:

I still do think as of right now [the most pressing issue] would be health and safety, but, um, it is affected by media and, um, information we spread about it.

—Respondent 39, partisan left

Summary of Interview Results

In summary, we conducted individual interviews with 15 people from different news consumption groups categorized according to their responses to our previous survey experiment (five from the partisan left, five from the partisan right, and five from the analytical skeptic group). We asked these interviewees the same set of questions that we asked the focus groups and generally found similar results. First, no interviewees described themselves in political terms at the start of these interviews. Second, both Russian memes appeared to elicit strong reactions from interviewees, leading some to make partisan assumptions about who would like the content. Third, most people assumed that Americans created the content. Fourth, most people understood the PSA warning them about this content, and most reacted positively, suggesting that the announcement was effective in the near term (see Appendix C for more details on research about the use of PSAs). Finally, the PSA appeared to be relevant for people after we explicitly told them the memes were sourced from Russia.

CHAPTER FIVE

Conclusion and Recommendations

We believe that Russia is effectively recycling our domestic partisanship at scale. In our three previous studies, we argued that Russia and its proxies exploit preexisting fault lines within U.S. society (Helmus et al., 2020; Marcellino et al., 2020; Posard et al., 2020). Put another way, Russia identifies who dislikes whom within the United States and then floods the information space with content to amplify these cleavages. The ultimate goal is to reduce the probability that people from different backgrounds will find consensus on issues of public concern. Thus, social divisions within domestic U.S. politics might create tactical opportunities for our adversaries to weaken our ability to form consensus on public issues.

This final report answers two questions:

1. What do people think and feel about partisan content that Russia and its proxies released on social media?
2. Could a PSA affect these views?

Our focus groups and interviews revealed three key findings, which we discuss here.

Most People Did Not Describe Themselves Politically, but Russian Content Tended to Elicit Partisan Reactions

The first question we asked participants in focus groups and interviews was to describe themselves. Despite purposefully selecting people who had reported having partisan views during a prior experiment, very few people in our sample used political terms to describe themselves. Instead, the vast majority used nonpolitical descriptors, such as their personality, hobbies, personal or professional roles, or demographic background. Although our sample is limited and nonrepresentative, these results might suggest that political leanings are not the most salient features for how people describe themselves, at least at first.

In general, we found additional evidence that Russian content works (Helmus et al., 2020). It elicits reactions from people on social issues that are sensitive for some.

When asked to describe their reactions, many people tended to make generalizations about other people—specifically, who would like or dislike this content. For example, one person assumed that the LGBT community, liberal politicians, the liberal media, then-Senator Kamala Harris, and her supporters would like the LGBT rights meme. In comparison, another respondent assumed that conservative, rural, working-class men who are middle-aged or older would like the Yosemite Sam meme.

Most People Assumed That Russian Content Was Created by Americans

Most of our participants thought that Americans created the Russian memes. This assumption was surprising for at least three reasons. First, our sample of focus group participants and interviewees were people who had completed an experiment on foreign disinformation two months earlier (in July 2020). During that experiment, participants viewed various memes that were created by Russia. Second, more than one-half of participants in this past experiment saw an intervention that told them that these memes were sourced from Russia, viewed a meme about media literacy, or viewed a video about media literacy. Of the 42 people in our sample, 27 of them (64.3 percent) had received one of these interventions. Third, Facebook displayed a warning when we posted the conservative Yosemite Sam meme stating that content in this meme contained false information. Facebook did not display this warning for the liberal LGBT rights meme that was also sourced from Russia, however. Despite seeing this Facebook warning about the Yosemite Sam meme, only two responses in our focus group raised the possibility that Russia might have created this content.

We suspect that the partisan content (that likely exploits respondents' preexisting views) in these Russian memes, coupled with the assumption that other Americans were creating this content, is what makes it particularly effective. Thus, mistaken attribution about the source of this content could be a key reason for its effectiveness on consumers.

After We Told People That the Memes Were Russian, the PSA Seemed to Be Effective for Most People

In general, the PSA appeared to be one effective tool for warning people about the broader strategy of foreign information efforts in the near term. Most participants in our focus groups and individual interviews appeared to understand this PSA. Few individuals we interviewed expressed a negative view of the PSA itself, and about one-third stated that foreign information efforts was a salient concern for them at the end of their interviews. The small number of individuals with a negative response to the PSA tended to express strong ideological and/or conspiratorial beliefs. It is unlikely that any PSA would be effective for those who already hold strong beliefs about election security, foreign information efforts, or political partisanship.

We found evidence that the PSA became particularly relevant to many people *after* we told them that both of the memes they had viewed were created by Russia and its proxies. Most people in our sample believed us, and none of these individuals expressed positive views about Russia and its proxies distributing partisan content—even if the content supported their own partisan beliefs. Thus, we believe that a repeated, generalized warning—coupled with specific examples that social media companies flag on their platforms—is likely to affect the largest number of people.

Recommendations

Using our analysis of responses from the limited number of people in our focus groups and interviews, we propose three recommendations, outlined in Figure 5.1, for governments to counter foreign information efforts targeting U.S. elections in the future.

Collect Open-Source Intelligence Early

Foreign information efforts are effective, in part, because they tend to elicit strong partisan reactions from those they target (Helmus et al., 2020). Furthermore, the audience tends to assume this foreign-sourced content is created by fellow Americans. Thus, the capacity to hide the source of this content via social media platforms gives foreign actors a tactical advantage when launching information efforts.

Recommendation 1: We recommend that Cal OES, in coordination with federal and private-sector partners, begin collecting open-source intelligence online to understand whom these bad actors are targeting. This collection should begin earlier rather than later in the election year. It should also be done throughout election years to ensure that Cal OES captures changes in tactics by foreign bad actors. We outlined a toolkit for capturing these changes in the second report of this series (Marcellino et al., 2020).

Figure 5.1
Overview of Recommendations

Release Public Service Announcements Several Times During Elections

We found evidence that a well-designed PSA from an official government source that uses a general and nonpartisan message is likely to be effective—at least, in the short term.

Recommendation 2: We recommend that Cal OES, in conjunction with the FBI and CISA, release a well-designed PSA with content that presents a general warning about the strategy of foreign information efforts. This PSA should meet at least three conditions:

1. It should focus on explaining general threats and avoid discussing any specific piece of online content, political party or issue, or subgroup of Americans. This general focus will reduce the likelihood that the public views a PSA, at least in the short term, as pushing a partisan agenda or targeting a group of Americans.
2. It should be well designed and clearly show that it comes from an official government source. Most of our focus group and interview participants recognized the FBI seal, though some people asked whether CISA was real. These questions are not surprising given that CISA is a relatively young agency that was formed within the Department of Homeland Security in 2018. Thus, we recommend that Cal OES, FBI, and CISA work together to release a single PSA that clearly shows that it is an approved government warning.
3. Importantly, this PSA should be released early in the election year. Cal OES and its stakeholders should work together to release a well-designed PSA early on and then continuously release this PSA on multiple online platforms during relevant elections. The PSA should be released in coordination with social media companies, so they can issue their own warnings about the sourcing of foreign content on their platforms.

Coordinate with Social Media Companies to Flag Foreign Political Content for Attribution

We found that the PSA became relevant for many people in our sample after we clearly told them that Russia and its proxies created the memes they had just viewed.

Recommendation 3: We recommend that Cal OES work with social media companies to flag the sourcing of foreign political content on their platforms. This flagging should occur at the same time that Cal OES and federal partners release a PSA warning about the general strategy behind known foreign information efforts. We note there is a need for additional research to understand what types of content, and how much of it, that social media companies should flag with warnings of attribution versus removing it all together. Nonetheless, we found evidence that a general warning from a PSA, coupled with specific examples independent of this PSA, are likely to be effective when displayed to people.

Use Case for Countering Foreign Information Efforts

To illustrate how Cal OES could implement our recommendations, we briefly discuss the 2020 presidential election as a use case. Figure 5.2 displays the cumulative total spent on campaigns by political candidates, PACs, and party committees between January 2019 and November 2020 as reported by the Federal Election Commission (undated). This figure shows that cumulative campaigning spending that was reported to the commission began to surpass $1 billion in September 2019. Using this apparent spending cycle, we propose that fall or early January is likely to be an optimal time for Cal OES to begin monitoring various social media platforms for foreign election interference.

Next, Cal OES could use the machine learning tools described in the second report of this series (Marcellino et al., 2020) on data from Twitter and other social media platforms throughout the election year. Using the results from this continuous analysis, Cal OES would then be able to (1) identify which communities are targets of foreign election interference, (2) develop a PSA directed at groups of people who are current and future targets and release it on social media platforms (i.e., Facebook, Twitter, Tik Tok), and then (3) coordinate with social media companies to have them flag the attribution of some political content at the same time the PSA is released.

Figure 5.2
Optimal Time in Campaign Cycle to Begin Monitoring for Foreign Disinformation (Cumulative Federal Campaign Spending, 2019–2020)

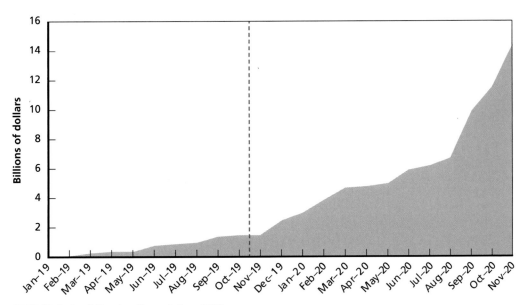

SOURCE: Federal Election Commission, 2020.
NOTE: This reflects money spent by candidates, political action committees, and party committees.

In conclusion, we believe that Russia is trying to recycle U.S. domestic partisanship at scale. A key reason that these attempts are successful is because people tend to mistakenly assume that their fellow Americans are creating and distributing online content that actually is coming from Russia. In the future, we should expect that our other adversaries will take notice of the effectiveness of Russia's efforts and might also try to exploit the fault lines that exist across the social and political fabric of the United States. This report outlines a strategy to warn people about these foreign efforts in a nonpartisan way.

Focus Group and Interview Guide

Here, we provide the guide used for the focus groups and individual interviews. The questions were asked of all participants, but not every question was answered; sometimes participants gave indirect responses that could not be coded, or they raised a different topic that they preferred to discuss.

A. General Questions—5 Minutes

First, I'm going to ask some general questions about you.

1. In a few words, how would you describe yourself?
   a. IF R ASKS: WHAT DO YOU MEAN?, ASK: How do you think your family members or friends would describe you, in a few words?
2. What are your personal political beliefs?
   a. IF NEEDED: Are you a member of a certain political party?
      ◦ IF NO: Why not?
      ◦ IF YES: Do you usually agree with that party's platforms and actions? Why or why not?
2. What type of news media do you view?
   a. IF NEEDED: Are there specific newspapers, TV channels, websites, radio stations, or other sources you learn about the news?
   b. What about online? How do you get news online?
3. What do you think is the most pressing issue occurring in your community right now?
   a. IF NEEDED (IF R ASKS): Your community would be your neighborhood, or the city you live in.

B. Impressions of Content—15 minutes

Meme 1

Next, we're going to show you some images—called *memes*—to understand your impressions. Can you please open the PDF document we emailed you? We're going to talk about the two images on the first page. First, let's talk about the image on the left.

1. What do you think of this meme?
   a. Why do you think that?
2. If you had to guess, who created this meme?
   a. IF NEEDED: Why do you think that?
3. How does this meme make you feel?
   a. Why?
4. How does this meme affect your views on politics?
   a. Why do you say that?

Meme 2

OK, now let's talk about the image on the right.

1. What do you think of this meme?
   a. Why do you think that?
2. If you had to guess, who created this meme?
   a. IF NEEDED: Why do you think that?
3. How does this meme make you feel?
   a. Why?
4. How does this meme affect your views on politics?
   a. Why do you say that?

Memes 1 and 2 Together

Now, I'm going to ask you some more questions about these memes; you can tell me what you think about *both* of them.

1. What types of people do you think would like these memes?
   a. Why?
   b. Do you think different people would like each one, or would people like both of them?
2. What types of people do you think would not like these memes?
   a. Why?
   b. Do you think different people would dislike each one?

3. Would you share these memes with others on social media?
   a. Why or why not?
   b. Who would you share it with?
   c. Are there people you wouldn't share it with? Who?
   d. IF NEEDED: What about the [other one/one on the left/one on the right]? Would you share that one?

C. Impressions of PSA—5 minutes

Now, we are going to show you an example of a public service message from the State of California. Can you please go to the second page of the PDF document?

1. What do you think of this public service announcement?
   a. Why do you think that?
2. Do you believe what it says?
   a. Why or why not?
3. How does this announcement make you feel?
   a. Why do you say that?
4. How does this announcement affect your views about politics?
   a. Why do you say that?
5. What types of people do you think would like this public service announcement?
   a. Why?
6. What types of people do you think would not like this announcement?
   a. Why?

D. Impressions of All Images—5 Minutes

OK, now I'm going to ask you some questions about all of the images we've discussed. Can you go to the third page of the document? This has the three images we have talked about so far.

1. Looking at them together, what do you think of these memes?
   a. How are they different?
   b. How are they similar?
   c. How do they make you feel?
2. Again, looking at all three memes together, how do they affect your views on politics?

E. This Is Russian Content—10 minutes

Ok, now I am going to tell you more about who created these memes. The first two memes that we discussed were created by the Russian government and people associated with the Russian government, according to research done by the United States Senate.[1]

1. Do you believe that Russia created these memes?
   a. Why or why not?
2. Does knowing the Russian government created these memes change your views of them?
   a. Why or why not?
3. The PSA—third image we talked about—was not created by the Russian government. Now that you know who created each image, does this change your views of the public service announcement we are showing you?
   a. Why or why not?
4. Returning back to a question we asked you earlier: What do you think is the most pressing issue occurring in your community right now?
   a. IF NEEDED: You can tell me the same thing you said before, or something different. There's no right or wrong answer.
   b. What types of people agree with you?
   c. What types of people disagree with you?

Those are all of the questions I have for you today. Thank you very much for your time, this has been very helpful. We will be emailing you a $50 Amazon gift code within the next week. Thanks again.

---

[1] This is an error that was discovered after the fact. Although both the U.S. House of Representatives, Permanent Select Committee on Intelligence, (2015–2017) and the U.S. Senate (2019) found evidence of Russian interference in the 2016 presidential elections, the House report listed the memes used in the focus groups and individual interviews.

Response Rates for Focus Groups and Interviews

This appendix describes the sample that we used for our focus groups and individual interviews. Participants in the former were not invited for the latter and vice versa. Figure B.1 displays our sampling strategy. This figure shows that a total of 1,529 respondents completed the second wave of the survey experiment from our third report of this series (for more details, see Helmus et al., 2020); 897 of these respondents (58.7 percent) volunteered on this survey to participate in a follow-up focus group or interview. Of these 897 respondents, we identified 106 people who met our criteria for inclusion in our focus groups (described in Chapter Two). We also identified 441 people who were eligible for individual interviews. We used quota sampling to recruit eligible participants, resulting in us contacting 58 people for our focus groups and 26 people for our interviews until we filled our quotas for each group (*n* = 27 people in our focus groups; *n* = 15 in our individual interview sample).

Figure B.1
Sampling Strategy for Focus Groups and Individual Interviews

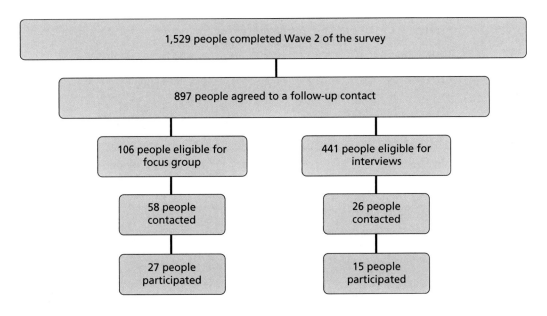

Table B.1 displays the number of volunteers invited to participate in the groups. We invited 58 of them to participate in online focus groups, with 27 people (46.6 percent) logging onto Facebook and participating. An additional 24 people (41.4 percent) did not respond to our follow-up interview request; six who were scheduled to participate in the focus group did not log on (10.3 percent), and one declined to participate after receiving the invitation (1.7 percent).

Table B.2 displays the total number of people who were invited to participate in individual interviews. We invited 26 people; 15 individuals (57.7 percent) completed an interview. Seven people (26.9 percent) did not respond to our invitation to participate, two were scheduled for an audio interview (7.7 percent) but did not log on for it, and two others responded after we completed our quota for interviews.

Table B.3 displays the types of memes and condition assignment that participants in this study completed during the survey experiment from our third task of this project (Helmus et al., 2020). During that experiment, respondents viewed various memes and then were randomly assigned to the control group, warning labels that notified them which memes were sourced from Russia, a meme warning them about foreign information efforts, or a media literacy video. Some, but not all, participants viewed

Table B.1
Sample Details of Focus Group Participants

Characteristic	Frequency	Percentage
Participated in focus group	27	46.5
Contacted for focus group; did not respond	24	41.4
Focus group scheduled but did not show up	6	10.3
Refused	1	1.7
Total contacts	58	99.0

NOTE: Percentages do not equal 100 percent because of rounding.

Table B.2
Sample Details of Individual Interviews

Characteristic	Frequency	Percentage
Participated in qualitative interviews	15	57.7
Contacted for interview; did not respond	7	26.9
Interview scheduled but did not show up	2	7.7
Responded after quota filled	2	7.7
Total contacts	26	100.0

Table B.3
Previous Survey Experience of Focus Group and Interview Participants

	Focus Groups		Individual Interviews	
Experience	Frequency	Percentage	Frequency	Percentage
Viewed memes				
Yosemite Sam	3	11.1	5	33.3
LGBT rights	1	3.7	1	6.7
Condition assignment				
Control group	12	44.4	3	20.0
Notified of Russian source	6	22.2	5	33.3
Meme warning	6	22.2	4	26.7
Video warning	3	11.1	3	20.0
Total	27		15	

the Yosemite Sam and LGBT rights meme that we used in the focus groups and individual interviews described in this report.

For each of our three focus groups, Facebook displayed a warning (shown by a screenshot in Figure B.2) only for the conservative Yosemite Sam meme. We do not have data on how many participants clicked the "See Why" button. Facebook did not display the same warning for the liberal LGBT rights meme. Both memes are sourced from Russia, according to reporting by the U.S. Congress (U.S. House of Representatives, Permanent Select Committee on Intelligence, 2015–2017).

Among our focus group participants, three (11.1 percent) had viewed the Yosemite Sam meme during the previous survey experiment; one (3.7 percent) had seen the LGBT rights meme. Twelve (44.4 percent) had been in the control condition in the previous survey experiment; six (22.2 percent) had seen a warning label about Russian memes; another six had viewed a media literacy meme; and three had viewed a media literacy video (11.1 percent).

Among our individual interviewees, five (33.3 percent) had viewed the Yosemite Sam meme during the previous survey experiment; one had viewed the LGBT rights meme (6.7 percent). Three (20 percent) had been in the control group during the past survey experiment, five had seen a warning about Russian sourcing while viewing memes (33.3 percent), four had viewed a media literacy meme (26.7 percent), and three had seen the media literacy video (20 percent).

Finally, the survey experiment told all respondents that they had viewed some memes sourced from Russia after they completed this instrument (for more details, see Helmus et al., 2020). Table B.3 illustrates this previous exposure.

Figure B.2
Screenshots of Facebook's Warning for the Yosemite Sam Meme

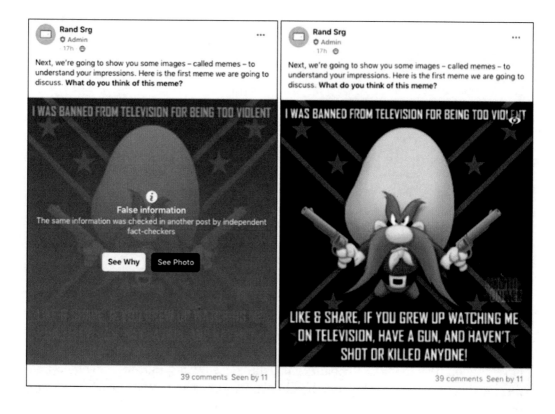

Relevant Literature

This appendix reviews both select research on ways to help people resist foreign disinformation and some relevant case studies. This research expands on our decision to test a PSA in our focus groups and one-on-one interviews.

Past Research on Resisting the Sway of Foreign Disinformation

The fact that participants did not suspect the memes we showed them were foreign disinformation—even after taking the survey that revealed some of the memes were Russian—led us to consider other methods that help consumers recognize and resist foreign disinformation. The research literature mentions emotional appeals, inoculation, public commitments, and forewarning of undue manipulative intent as ways to help consumers resist foreign disinformation. Cal OES might be able to use this research to guide public communications campaigns during election seasons. We provide a brief synopsis of each method.

Public communications: First, it is important to note that public communications campaigns rely on gaining the consumer's attention. Research by Pfau et al. (2001) points out that drawing attention can more easily be done by engaging consumers emotionally, which often means addressing topics that consumers care about. PSAs or a public communications campaign to protect elections might benefit from creating emotionally relevant materials to capture the interest of consumers.

Inoculation: *Inoculation theory* helps people resist persuasion. Applied to combating foreign disinformation, an inoculation would warn consumers of foreign disinformation, expose them to a weakened piece of persuasive foreign disinformation (similar to the way that weak antigens are exposed to a vaccine), and then refute the foreign disinformation (similar to creating antibodies). Inoculation has been used since the 1960s in public health, political campaigns, communications, and other fields (Compton, Jackson, and Dimmock, 2016, Table 1; Cook, Lewandowsky, and Ecker, 2017, and Lessne and Didou, 1987). A meta-analysis of 54 inoculation studies reported that inoculated subjects showed resistance to persuasion for an average of 14 days after inoculation (Banas and Rains, 2010). If the inoculated did not encounter the foreign disinformation for which they were inoculated, their resistance began to decline after 14 days. Constructing messaging to warn and inoculate Californians against the foreign disinformation tactics they are most likely to experience might have a long-lasting impact and help Californians better resist foreign disinformation.

Public commitments: Public commitments are also powerful in helping consumers resist foreign disinformation. Research shows that when people publicly commit to something—even small things, such as "liking" a page or signing a petition—they more strongly resist persuasion to act against their public commitment (Cialdini, 2008; Nyer and Gopinath, 2006). A PSA about election security against foreign disinformation might ask people to "like" or follow election safety pages, or to "like" or share that they have committed to taking small, nonpartisan steps toward resisting foreign disinformation, such as checking sources or looking up suspicious claims.

Forewarning of undue manipulative intent: Research has shown that forewarning consumers of undue manipulative intent from foreign disinformation helps them resist it better than no warning at all (Sagarin et al., 2002). However, forewarning of specific content is not recommended and can even backfire by eliciting the opposite of the intended behavior. However, forewarning consumers of the general intent of some foreign governments or foreign news sources to manipulate the election could help them recognize and resist foreign disinformation.

Insights from Other Case Studies and Research

Competing in the information environment is more difficult for democratic governments than for more-autocratic ones. Chief foreign U.S. adversaries in the information sphere—e.g., Russia, China, Iran—are autocratic regimes that exercise greater control over media and media narratives than is possible in a democratic government with freedom of the press. However, other democracies have modeled organizations that affect the information sphere and counter efforts from autocratic regimes. The Ukraine Crisis Media Center (UCMC) provides one example of a democratic institution able to compete with an autocratic opponent. Formed in 2014 in response to Russian aggression and foreign disinformation efforts in Ukraine, the UCMC builds public trust through daily news briefings and provides a platform for frequent updates, panels, and broadcasts from officials all over Ukraine and abroad (de Jong et al., 2017; Haring, 2019). UCMC is the seat of Ukraine's One Voice policy, which coordinates a single Ukrainian narrative and broadcasts it over several media channels. This competes against unified Russian narratives that are also broadcast over several media channels (Walker, 2015).

In the United States, the newly formed Partnership for Countering Influence Operations, a part of the Carnegie Endowment for International Peace, is a U.S. partnership among businesses, social media companies, international experts, and academia that research and create best practices for countering influence operations (Carnegie Endowment for International Peace, undated). Other partnerships might also model cooperatives useful to responding to foreign disinformation in a democratic society.

With or without a public-private partnership for competing in influence operations, research shows that simple things can improve the quality of influential messages. Although our participants mostly reported favorable results after reading the PSA, they were in an experimental setting and complied with instructions to read the PSA. In a natural environment, consumers might not take the time to read the full PSA in the current format. Research on influence supports authority as an influential factor in a message (Cialdini, 2008), hence the official seal of the FBI is one influential aspect of the existing PSA. Additionally, research supports unity, social proof, liking, and shareability as influential features (Cialdini, 2008; Cialdini, 2016; van der Linden et al., 2017). *Unity* means something is more influential if it represents or comes from a group that the person feels a part of. Emphasizing that some information efforts are foreign campaigns against "us Americans" might help create an influential sense of unity. Likewise, *social proof* entails something having more influence if other people already support it. Social media is well suited to creating social proof because most platforms provide a way to "like" a post—validation that increase the post's influence. Liking means a message is more influential if it is attractive or conveyed by someone who is attractive or similar to the consumer. Finally, research shows messages supporting resistance to foreign disinformation can spread in the same way that foreign disinformation spreads: virally. Making a PSA attractive and sharable might increase the likelihood that consumers will read it, pass it on, and increase the PSA's effectiveness.

References

Amazon, "Amazon Transcribe," webpage, undated. As of February 2, 2020:
https://aws.amazon.com/transcribe/

Banas, John A., and Stephen A. Rains, "A Meta-Analysis of Research on Inoculation Theory," *Communication Monographs*, Vol. 77, No. 3, September 22, 2010, pp. 281–311.

Carnegie Endowment for International Peace, "Partnership for Countering Influence Operations," webpage, undated. As of December 11, 2020:
https://carnegieendowment.org/specialprojects/counteringinfluenceoperations

Cialdini, Robert B., *Influence: Science and Practice*, 5th ed., Glenview, Ill.: Scott Foresman and Company, 2008.

Cialdini, Robert, *Pre-Suasion: A Revolutionary Way to Influence and Persuade*, New York: Simon and Schuster, 2016.

Compton, Josh, Ben Jackson, and James A. Dimmock, "Persuading Others to Avoid Persuasion: Inoculation Theory and Resistant Health Attitudes," *Frontiers in Psychology*, Vol. 7, No. 122, February 9, 2016.

Cook, John, Stephan Lewandowsky, and Ullrich K. H. Ecker, "Neutralizing Misinformation Through Inoculation: Exposing Misleading Argumentation Techniques Reduces Their Influence," *PLoS ONE*, Vol. 12, No. 5, May 5, 2017.

Dawkins, Richard, *The Selfish Gene*, Oxford, UK: Oxford University Press, 1976.

de Jong, Sijbren, Tim Sweijs, Katarina Kertysova, Roel Bos, Rob de Rave, Pieter Bindt, Katharine Klacansky, Mateus Mendonça Oliveira, Paul Verhagen, Henry Fersko, et al., *Inside the Kremlin House of Mirrors: How Liberal Democracies Can Counter Russian Foreign Disinformation and Societal Interference*, Netherlands: Hague Centre for Strategic Studies, 2017.

de Vries, Han, Marc N. Elliott, David E. Kanouse, and Stephanie S. Teleki, "Using Pooled Kappa to Summarize Interrater Agreement across Many Items," *Field Methods*, Vol. 20, No. 3, August 2008, pp. 272–282.

Ewing, Philip, "Russian Targeted U.S. Racial Divisions Long Before 2016 and Black Lives Matter," National Public Radio, October 30, 2017. As of December 8, 2020:
https://www.npr.org/2017/10/30/560042987/
russians-targeted-u-s-racial-divisions-long-before-2016-and-black-lives-matter

FBI and CISA—*See* Federal Bureau of Investigation and Cybersecurity and Infrastructure Security Agency.

Federal Bureau of Investigation and Cybersecurity and Infrastructure Security Agency, "Foreign Actors and Cybercriminals Likely to Spread Foreign Disinformation Regarding 2020 Election Results," public service announcement, September 22, 2020. As of December 2, 2020: https://www.ic3.gov/Media/Y2020/PSA200922

Federal Election Commission, "Campaign Finance Data," webpage, undated. As of December 8, 2020: https://www.fec.gov/data/browse-data/?tab=spending

Haring, Melinda, "Their Brand Is Crisis," Atlantic Council, blog post, March 5, 2019.

Helmus, Todd C., James V. Marrone, Marek N. Posard, and Danielle Schlang, *Russian Propaganda Hits Its Mark: Experimentally Testing the Impact of Russian Propaganda and Counter-Interventions*, Santa Monica, Calif.: RAND Corporation, RR-A704-3, 2020. As of December 8, 2020: https://www.rand.org/pubs/research_reports/RRA704-3.html

Lessne, Greg J., and Nicholas M. Didou, Jr., "Inoculation Theory and Resistance to Persuasion in Marketing," *Psychology & Marketing*, Vol. 4, No. 2, Summer 1987, pp. 157–165.

Marcellino, William, Christian Johnson, Marek N. Posard, and Todd C. Helmus, *Foreign Interference in the 2020 Election: Tools for Detecting Online Election Interference*, Santa Monica, Calif.: RAND Corporation, RR-A704-2, 2020. As of December 8, 2020: https://www.rand.org/pubs/research_reports/RRA704-2.html

McCrae, James, "Meme Marketing: How Brands are Speaking a New Consumer Language," *Forbes*, May 8, 2017. As of August 20, 2020: https://www.forbes.com/sites/forbescommunicationscouncil/2017/05/08/meme-marketing-how-brands-are-speaking-a-new-consumer-language/?sh=17dd077137f5

Nyer, Prashanth U., and Mahesh Gopinath, "The Effect of Public Commitment on Resistance to Persuasion: Preliminary Findings," in Silvia Gonzalez and David Luna, eds., *Latin American Advances in Consumer Research*, Vol. 1, Duluth, Minn.: Association for Consumer Research, 2006, pp. 52–53.

Paul, Christopher, and Miriam Matthews, *The Russian "Firehose of Falsehood" Propaganda Model: Why It Might Work and Options to Counter It*, Santa Monica, Calif.: RAND Corporation, PE-198-OSD, 2016. As of January 12, 2021: https://www.rand.org/pubs/perspectives/PE198.html

Pfau, Michael, Erin Alison Szabo, Jason Anderson, Joshua Morrill, Jessica Zubric, and Hua-Hsin Wan, "The Role and Impact of Affect in the Process of Resistance to Persuasion," *Human Communication Research*, Vol. 27, No. 2, April 2001, pp. 216–252.

Posard, Marek N., Marta Kepe, Hilary Reininger, James V. Marrone, Todd C. Helmus, and Jordan R. Reimer, *From Consensus to Conflict: Understanding Foreign Measures Targeting U.S. Elections*, Santa Monica, Calif.: RAND Corporation, RR-A704-1, 2020. As of December 8, 2020: https://www.rand.org/pubs/research_reports/RRA704-1.html

Ring, Trudy, "Russian Trolls' Fake LGBT Facebook Group Was Very Popular," *Advocate*, May 11, 2018. As of December 17, 2020: https://www.advocate.com/politics/2018/5/11/russian-trolls-fake-lgbt-facebook-group-was-very-popular

Sagarin, Brad J., Robert B. Cialdini, William E. Rice, and Sherman B. Serna, "Dispelling the Illusion of Invulnerability: The Motivations and Mechanisms of Resistance to Persuasion," *Journal of Personality and Social Psychology*, Vol. 83, No. 3, 2002, pp. 526–541.

Thomas, Timothy L., "Russia's Reflexive Control Theory and the Military," *Journal of Slavic Military Studies*, Vol. 17, 2004, pp. 237–256.

U.S. House of Representatives, Permanent Select Committee on Intelligence, "Social Media Advertisements," webpage, 2015–2017 (assorted). As of August 30, 2020:
https://intelligence.house.gov/social-media-content/social-media-advertisements.htm

U.S. Senate, Select Committee on Intelligence, *Report of the Select Committee on Intelligence United States Senate on Russian Active Measures Campaigns and Interference in the 2016 U.S. Election*, Vol. 1, *Russian Efforts Against Election Infrastructure with Additional Views*, 116th Congress, Report 116-290, 2019. As of July 29, 2020:
https://www.intelligence.senate.gov/sites/default/files/documents/Report_Volume1.pdf

———, *Report of the Select Committee on Intelligence United States Senate on Russian Active Measures Campaigns and Interference in the 2016 U.S. Election*, Vol. 2: *Russia's Use of Social Media with Additional Views*, 116th Congress, Report 116-290, 2019. As of July 29, 2020:
https://www.intelligence.senate.gov/sites/default/files/documents/Report_Volume2.pdf

———, *Report of the Select Committee on Intelligence United States Senate on Russian Active Measures Campaigns and Interference in the 2016 U.S. Election*, Vol. 5: *Counterintelligence Threats and Vulnerabilities*, 116th Congress, Report 116-290, 2019. As of August 27, 2020:
https://www.intelligence.senate.gov/sites/default/files/documents/report_volume5.pdf

van der Linden, Sander, Edward Maibach, John Cook, Anthony Leiserowitz, and Stephen Lewandowsky, "Inoculating Against Misinformation," *Science*, Vol. 358, No. 6367, December 1, 2017, pp. 1141–1142.

Walker, Vivian S., *Case Study 331: State Narratives in Complex Media Environments: The Case of Ukraine*, Washington, D.C.: Institute for the Study of Diplomacy at Georgetown University, 2015.

Zaller, John, and Stanley Feldman, "A Simple Theory of the Survey Response: Answering Questions Versus Revealing Preferences," *American Journal of Political Science*, Vol. 36, No. 3, August 1992, pp. 579–616.